SAGRADA FAMÍLIA

Stone, Light, and Gaudí's Unfinished Masterpiece

Inside Barcelona's Most Extraordinary Basilica

PRANAV PANDYA

SAGRADA FAMÍLIA
Stone, Light, and Gaudí's Unfinished Masterpiece
Inside Barcelona's Most Extraordinary Basilica

Copyright © 2025 PRANAV PANDYA
All rights reserved.

No part of this publication may be reproduced, stored in a retrieval system, or transmitted in any form or by any means, electronic, mechanical, photocopying, recording, or otherwise, except in the case of brief quotations used in reviews or scholarly works.

This book is a work of nonfiction. Every effort has been made to ensure the accuracy of the information presented. The author and publisher assume no responsibility for errors, omissions, or changes occurring after publication.

Special Note on Visual Plates: This edition features bespoke visual plates, each created exclusively for this volume. These plates have been designed with meticulous attention to detail, capturing both the artistry and the spiritual intent of Gaudí's vision, from the unfinished façades to the intricate vaulting and interior lightscapes. Each plate is an original creation for this book and is protected under international copyright law.

First Edition Independently Published

On the previous page: A serene aerial view of the Sagrada Família bathed in soft pastel hues, its towers rising gracefully above Barcelona's skyline.

TABLE OF CONTENTS

Acknowledgements

About This Book

Prologue – Entering Light

Chapter 1 - Gaudi's Grammer of Nature

Chapter 2 - From Stone to Sky

Chapter 3 - The Three Facades

Chapter 4 - The Forest Within

Chapter 5 – Windows of Fire and Sea

Chapter 6 - Sound & Space

Chapter 7 - Towers of Faith

Chapter 8 - The Crypt & Lower Realms

Chapter 9 - Symbols in Stone and Glass

Chapter 10 - Gaudi's Vision Realized

Chapter 11 - Photographer's Map

Epilogue – The Eternal Work in Progress

Antoni Gaudi – The Architect of God's Geometry

The Architectural Language of Antoni Gaudi

Barcelona – City of Light, Sea, and Stone

Catalonia – Land Between Mountains and Sea

Spain – A Land of Many Worlds

Appendix A – Visual Glossary

Appendix B – Timeline & Milestones

Sources & Citations

Further Reading & Exploration

About The Author

Visual Plates

ACKNOWLEDGEMENTS

This book was shaped by many hands and hearts. My deepest gratitude goes to the historians, architects, artisans, and conservationists whose tireless devotion to the Sagrada Família keeps Gaudí's dream alive. Their skill and perseverance are reminders that beauty and meaning can outlast generations.

To the archivists and curators who opened the doors to drawings, models, and rare photographs, your generosity enriched this work beyond measure, ensuring every detail rests on a foundation of authenticity.

Special thanks to the artists and image creators who collaborated on the bespoke plates within these pages. Each one is more than an illustration; it is a crafted interpretation of Gaudí's genius, capturing both the precision of his geometry and the poetry of his vision.

To my friends and family, who indulged countless conversations about façades, vaulting, and bell towers, and who reminded me to simply stand back and marvel, thank you for your patience and encouragement.

Finally, to the city of Barcelona: your streets, plazas, and skyline continue to cradle this unfinished symphony of stone. The basilica belongs to the world, but it is your heartbeat that keeps it alive.

In deep gratitude,

Pranav Pandya

ABOUT THIS BOOK

Step inside the soaring heart of Barcelona's most beloved landmark, the Sagrada Família, and witness the story of a masterpiece more than a century in the making.

This is not just an architectural guide; it is a journey into the vision of Antoni Gaudí, the genius who fused faith, nature, and mathematics into stone. Through richly woven storytelling and exclusive full-page visual plates, you will see the basilica as never before, from the sunlit kaleidoscope of its stained glass to the gravity-defying towers that crown the Catalan skyline.

Each chapter invites you closer to the soul of this living cathedral: the intricate façades alive with biblical scenes, the forest of stone columns reaching heavenward, and the spiritual symbolism hidden in every carving. Along the way, you'll encounter Gaudí's groundbreaking techniques, from upside-down string models to his belief in nature as the ultimate blueprint, and discover how modern artisans are carrying his work into the future.

These pages bridge past and present, dream and reality, culminating in a visionary rendering of the completed basilica, all eighteen towers and every decorative flourish in place, offering a rare glimpse of what will one day stand in full glory.

Whether you are an architecture devotee, a traveler longing for Barcelona, or simply a dreamer inspired by human creativity, *Sagrada Família* will leave you awed, and forever changed, by one of the world's most extraordinary creations.

On the next page: A digital image capturing the Sagrada Família's interior, where sunlight pours through intricate stained glass, bathing the space in a kaleidoscope of vivid colors.

PROLOGUE

Entering Light

From the heart of Barcelona, a forest of stone rises into the sky, its towers reaching like living spires that change with the shifting light. The Sagrada Família is more than a landmark, it is a vision given form, a prayer in progress, and perhaps the most extraordinary basilica ever attempted.

At first sight, it resists definition. The eye meets shapes both ancient and strange: façades alive with sculpture, towers crowned with mosaic pinnacles that catch the sun, and curves that follow no straight-edged tradition. Everything flows with the quiet logic of nature, the rhythm Gaudí spent a lifetime studying and translating into architecture.

Approach from the east in early morning, and the Nativity Façade glows with abundance, vines curling, animal's mid-step, angels leaning forward in welcome. By evening, the Passion Façade answers with severity: bone-like columns, stark shadows, and a stripped, solemn beauty. Between them waits the unfinished Glory Façade, still shrouded in scaffolding, still whispering of what is yet to come.

Step inside, and the world changes. Columns rise like trees, branching into vaults that filter daylight from skylights high above. Stained glass turns the air into a living tapestry, ocean blues in the morning, molten reds and golds at sunset. Time slows. The space gathers you in, as if light itself were part of the structure.

The Sagrada Família is unfinished, and perhaps that is its most fitting truth. For more than a century, it has grown stone by stone, carried forward by countless hands and hearts. It is a work belonging to no single lifetime, yet to every life that has touched it. Gaudí knew this.

He planted a seed, trusting that others would nurture it with faith, craft, and patience. Today, as you stand beneath its rising towers and watch the light move across its walls, you become part of that same long story, a story of stone, light, and an unfinished masterpiece.

CHAPTER 1

Gaudí's Grammar of Nature

To understand the Sagrada Família, you must first understand the language in which it is written. Gaudí did not design with lines and measurements alone; he composed with the vocabulary of nature. His grammar was not that of rigid human rules, but of curves found in seashells, the branching of trees, and the flowing geometry of rivers and wind.

As a boy in the Catalan countryside, illness often kept him still. Stillness sharpened his attention. He noticed how a leaf's veins guided water, how a snail's shell spiraled inward with mathematical precision, how sunlight shifted over stone through the hours. These quiet observations became the foundation of his design philosophy, that nature was the greatest teacher, and that architecture should work with, not against, its principles.

When Gaudí took over the Sagrada Família in 1883, he inherited the beginnings of a conventional neo-Gothic church. But he saw an opportunity to create something entirely his own, a structure shaped by the same laws that govern living things. Columns would grow like tree trunks, branching to support the vaults without heavy buttresses. Arches would follow the natural catenary curve of a hanging chain, the strongest and most graceful form for bearing weight. Towers would taper like mountain peaks, their summits crowned with mosaics that glistened like dew at dawn.

In Gaudí's hands, beauty and structure were inseparable. Color, light, and organic lines were not ornament but part of the building's essence. Every sculptural detail was a lesson, every space an invitation to see deeper. He built with the conviction that form should emerge naturally from function, just as in nature.

In his workshop, Gaudí relied less on paper plans than on physical models. Weighted strings revealed perfect curves when left to gravity; inverted, they became arches that could stand for centuries. Sunlight traced its path across miniature façades, guiding window placement and shaping the dance of light within the basilica. He trusted the mathematics of nature more than the straightedge of convention.

The result is a building that reads like a living text, one written in stone and glass, illuminated by the changing light. Its façades and towers are sentences, its sculptural flourishes the words, and the entire basilica the story. To walk through it is to read a language older than any script, one that speaks directly to the senses. In Gaudí's grammar, the Sagrada Família is a poem that will take more than a century to finish, yet even unfinished, it speaks with perfect fluency.

CHAPTER 2

From Stone to Sky

The Sagrada Família is not the product of a single lifetime. It is a work carried forward by generations, each adding their stone to a slow, deliberate ascent. From its first foundation trench to the highest mosaic-crowned spire, the basilica's story is one of vision meeting persistence, century after century.

When Gaudí took over in 1883, only the crypt was complete. The original neo-Gothic plan left by Francisco de Paula del Villar was serviceable but unremarkable. Gaudí saw something else: a basilica whose very bones would echo the structures of nature, where geometry and faith could rise together into forms the world had never seen.

The early years were painstaking. Funds arrived in small bursts, and every block of stone demanded hours of handwork. Gaudí devoted himself to the Nativity Façade, determined to finish at least one part that would bear his full signature. He worked among the scaffolding, clay models, and dusty workshops, shifting a figure's position or adjusting a curve as the light changed. Stone from Montjuïc arrived in rough blocks, their grain felt beneath the mason's hand before the first cut was made.

By 1926, when Gaudí died after being struck by a tram, less than a quarter of the basilica had been built. The Nativity Façade stood as a testament to his vision, its towers already visible across the city, but much of the site was still open to the sky.

The decades that followed were turbulent. Civil war damaged parts of the workshop, destroying some of Gaudí's models and plans. What survived often came in fragments, reconstructed like a giant puzzle by architects and artisans who saw their work as an act of devotion. Each generation faced the challenge of interpreting his vision with the tools of their own time.

In the present day, cranes rise among the towers as naturally as the pinnacles themselves. Laser-cutting machines shape stone with precision Gaudí could scarcely imagine, yet the final carving and fitting still depend on human skill. Old-world craftsmanship and modern engineering meet in every block and joint.

From its roots in the crypt to its tallest spire, the Sagrada Família has always been a vertical journey, an unbroken act of building upward. Every stone set is part of a larger gesture, a slow reaching toward the sky. And when the day comes that the last piece is placed, the basilica will not simply have been completed; it will have fulfilled a century-long climb from earth to light.

CHAPTER 3

The Three Façades

The Sagrada Família tells its story in three immense stone pages, each a façade with its own voice, mood, and message. They are more than entrances; they are narratives in relief, gateways that prepare the visitor for the journey within. Together, they trace a cycle as old as the Christian faith, birth, death, and resurrection, each stage carved into the face of the basilica.

The Nativity Façade greets the rising sun. It was the first to be built, the only one completed largely under Gaudí's direct supervision, and it bears his presence in every curve and cluster of detail. The stone overflows with life: scenes from Christ's birth unfold among vines, flowers, animals, and angels. Figures seem close enough to touch, leaning outward to welcome. Morning light falls on these carvings so that they appear to glow from within, a daily resurrection of the new day's promise.

Facing the opposite direction, the Passion Façade meets the setting sun and offers a stark contrast. Where the Nativity is lush and abundant, the Passion is stripped bare. Its surfaces are taut and angular, its figures, sculpted decades later by Josep Maria Subirachs, are gaunt, their forms rigid with sorrow. Deep shadows slice across the stone as evening approaches, intensifying the sense of suffering and sacrifice. This is not a façade meant to comfort. It confronts, reminding visitors of the cost at the heart of the story.

The Glory Façade, still taking shape, will face south toward the midday sun. It is planned as the grandest of the three, the final chapter of the basilica's narrative. Here will be carved the themes of resurrection, eternal life, and humanity's union with the divine. Drawn from Gaudí's surviving sketches and interpreted by contemporary architects, it will one day become the main entrance, guiding visitors through a vast symbolic threshold into the heart of the basilica. Even in its unfinished state, its arches and openings suggest an ascent into light.

Each façade speaks in a distinct dialect of Gaudí's language. The Nativity welcomes with joy, the Passion confronts with truth, and the Glory will one day lift the gaze to hope. Before a visitor even crosses the threshold, the building has already told its story, a spiritual journey written in stone.

CHAPTER 4

The Forest Within

Stepping inside the Sagrada Família is like entering another world. The noise of the city falls away, replaced by a quiet that carries the soft echo of footsteps and murmured voices. Above, light streams down through windows and skylights, shifting as clouds drift and the sun makes its slow arc. The air seems touched by color, changing hue with each passing moment.

Gaudí imagined the nave as a forest, and here that vision becomes reality. Columns rise from the floor like trees, branching high into a canopy of stone. No two are the same. Some stand broad and solid, others slender and soaring, each branching pattern a careful study in both form and function. Their shapes are not just beautiful; they bear the weight of the vaults as effortlessly as trunks carry leaves.

Light filters through this stone canopy much like sunlight through leaves. Skylights pour illumination into the nave, while the stained glass sends pools of color drifting across the floor and climbing the columns. Morning brings cool blues and greens from the east windows; by late afternoon, reds and golds blaze from the west, filling the air with warmth.

The plan of the space draws you forward. The central nave and side aisles guide the gaze toward the altar, while the vertical lines of the columns pull it upward without effort. The acoustics soften every sound; a whisper seems to float rather than fade, as though the stone itself is listening. Touching a column reveals the cool smoothness of the stone, its surface shaped by hand yet retaining the quiet texture of its grain.

Moving through the nave is like walking through changing light. You pass from shadow into radiance, each step a shift in mood. Symbols and patterns carved at the base of the columns speak of both nature and scripture, anchoring the soaring space in meaning.

Gaudí's forest is not meant to overwhelm but to embrace. The proportions are vast, yet they hold the human scale close. From the nave to the transept crossing, the space opens slowly, revealing more light, more height, and more air. Here, stone becomes sky, and sky descends into stone, until the boundary between the two is no longer clear.

CHAPTER 5

Windows of Fire and Sea

Light inside the Sagrada Família is not still. It moves, changes, and transforms the very air. In this basilica, stained glass is not decoration; it is an instrument through which the sun composes its own symphony.

On the eastern side, where morning breaks, the glass holds the colors of water. Blues in every depth, from pale aquamarine to midnight indigo, are threaded with greens that recall forest leaves, seaweed in a current, or fields just after rain. As the sun rises, these hues wash over the nave, bringing a calm, cool clarity that feels like a slow intake of breath.

By afternoon, the west side burns with fire. The glass here blazes with amber, gold, crimson, and deep orange. When the sun drops low, its light pours through with an intensity that seems almost physical, igniting columns and floor in molten color. The air itself appears to glow, as if the basilica were lit from within.

The colors do not remain in the windows. They spill outward, climbing the stone like climbing vines, pooling on the floor in shifting shapes. A few steps can take a visitor from deep blue shadow into a burst of gold. The effect is never the same twice. Clouds, seasons, and the slow turn of the day change the composition moment by moment. The basilica becomes a clock without numbers, its hours marked in color.

Gaudí imagined these windows as more than beauty. Their patterns suggest rippling water, rays of light, petals unfurling, and nature distilled into glass. Biblical themes are woven in, so that the light carries story as well as color.

The east whispers of the morning sea; the west roars with the fire of day's end. Between them lies the shifting tide of hours, the meeting of water and flame, coolness and heat, beginning and completion. In their glow, the Sagrada Família breathes.

CHAPTER 6

Sound & Space

The first thing you notice is the quiet. Not absence, but presence, a stillness that gathers every sound and holds it. In the Sagrada Família, even a single step carries, a whisper lingers, and the pause between notes feels like part of the music.

Gaudí understood that a sacred building must be shaped for the ear as well as the eye. The height of the vaults, the branching of the columns, the curves of the walls, all serve to carry sound without losing clarity. Voices travel with warmth, rounded by the space, yet remain distinct. Reverberation enriches without obscuring. It is architecture tuned like an instrument.

At the heart of this sound is the organ. Its polished pipes rise in gleaming ranks, catching fragments of color from the stained glass. When the music begins, the sound does not come from one place but seems to bloom everywhere at once. Deep notes anchor the air, bright reeds sparkle like midday light, and quiet flutes drift like wind through leaves.

Future plans imagine more than one organ, placed throughout the basilica, able to speak together. Music would then flow from every direction, wrapping visitors in a tapestry of sound as intricate as the carvings on the façades.

Yet the voice of the Sagrada Família is not only in instruments or choir. It lives in the rustle of a coat, the creak of a wooden pew, the faint shuffle of feet over stone. Even the muffled breath of the city beyond the doors enters changed, softened, and made part of the whole. The building listens, and in return it answers with resonance.

Here, sound becomes a form of light. It moves through space, touches the stone, and reaches upward, vanishing into the canopy of vaults. To see this place is one thing. To hear it, to feel it in the air and in your chest, is to understand that Gaudí built not only a sanctuary for the eye, but a sanctuary for the soul.

CHAPTER 7

Towers of Faith

Seen from across Barcelona, the towers of the Sagrada Família rise like a cluster of stone flames, their tips catching the sun. Up close, they are more than feats of engineering, they are a chorus of symbols, each one a vertical offering in Gaudí's great act of devotion.

Gaudí imagined eighteen towers in all: twelve for the apostles, four for the evangelists, one for the Virgin Mary, and the tallest for Jesus Christ. Together, they form a hierarchy in stone, a vertical reflection of the heavenly order.

The four evangelist towers stand around the central spire, each crowned with its ancient emblem, a man for Matthew, a lion for Mark, an ox for Luke, an eagle for John. These symbols, rendered in vibrant mosaics, blaze under the midday sun and glow softly when lit at night, like beacons marking the four directions.

Beside the central spire rises the Tower of the Virgin Mary, graceful and serene, topped with a twelve-pointed star. At night, the star shines high above the city, a fixed point of light in the urban sky, both landmark and guide.

At the heart of them all, the Jesus Christ Tower climbs higher than any other, set to reach 172.5 meters when complete. It will be crowned with a great cross, its arms aligned with the compass, sheathed in ceramic and glass to scatter sunlight in all directions. Gaudí, mindful of nature's precedence, ensured it would stand lower than Montjuïc hill, keeping human creation beneath the work of the earth.

The towers are alive to their surroundings. Narrow openings let the wind pass through in shifting tones; their textured surfaces break and catch the light so that no two hours look the same. From the ground, they draw the gaze upward in a slow ascent. Each has its own meaning, yet together they form a single upward motion, faith made visible, always reaching, always rising.

CHAPTER 8

The Crypt & Lower Realms

Beneath the blaze of stained glass and the towering forest of columns lies a quieter world. To enter the crypt of the Sagrada Família is to step into the roots of the basilica, the place where its story began, and where Gaudí himself now rests.

This was the first part of the building to be completed, designed by Francisco de Paula del Villar before Gaudí assumed the project in 1883. Its architecture is more traditional: a Latin cross plan, low arches, and thick walls that hold the coolness of stone. Light seeps in through small windows, dim and golden, lending the space the hush of an older church.

When Gaudí took over, his touch reached even here. He added sculptural flourishes and softened the geometry to echo the organic harmony of his larger vision. Over the decades, the crypt became a living space of worship, still used today for services that gather in the intimate glow of candlelight rather than the blaze of the nave.

In a side chapel rests Gaudí's tomb. Modest in scale, it bears his name in Catalan beneath a sculpture of Christ. Visitors often stand silently before it, some in prayer, and others simply in respect. The humility of the grave contrasts with the scale of the work above, as if to remind that greatness can grow from simplicity.

Nearby, the museum and workshop spaces display the fragile survivors of Gaudí's working life, scale models reconstructed from shards after the devastation of the Spanish Civil War, drawings that chart the basilica's evolving form, and photographs that preserve its progress through the years. These rooms feel like an archive of both vision and perseverance.

Here in the lower levels, you feel the weight of the structure overhead, not as a burden, but as a reassurance. The crypt is the basilica's root system, unseen yet essential, holding the dream steady while it rises. In its shadowed quiet, the upward reach of towers and columns feels all the more miraculous, as if the whole vast work above were being nourished from this still, stone heart.

CHAPTER 9

Symbols in Stone and Glass

Symbols are the Sagrada Família's second language, as present as its stone and glass. Gaudí filled the basilica with them so that every visitor, believer or not, could encounter layers of meaning. Some reveal themselves instantly; others hide in plain sight, waiting for a slower gaze.

On the façades, the message is bold. The Nativity overflows with life, flowers, fruit, animals, and angels woven into scenes of Christ's birth, the abundance of creation carved in joyous detail. The Passion stands in deliberate contrast: stripped of ornament, its sharp lines and deep shadows capture the stark truth of suffering and sacrifice. The Glory, still rising, will tell of resurrection and eternal life, a stone vision of hope.

Inside, the language grows more intricate. The forest-like columns are crowned with capitals carved in the likeness of plants from the Holy Land, linking the basilica to the landscapes of scripture. Their branching forms speak both of the spread of the Gospel and the branching logic of living nature. In Gaudí's world, the sacred and the natural are never separate.

The stained glass carries the story in light. Morning rises through blues and greens, evoking water and creation; afternoon falls in reds and golds, the fire of fulfillment. The day's passage becomes a living narrative, from the cool clarity of beginning to the warmth of completion, mirrored in the liturgical year.

Even the smallest elements carry significance. The Passion doors bear the words of the Gospels in raised lettering, so scripture itself forms the threshold. On the Nativity side, lizards and birds nestle among carved leaves, a reminder that all creation praises the divine. Numbers appear in deliberate sequences, referencing biblical passages, hidden for those who care to seek them.

For Gaudí, a grapevine was both a plant and the Eucharist; a spiral shell, both a natural marvel and a sign of life's unfolding. He wove these meanings together so that the basilica could be read like an illuminated manuscript, one written in stone, glass, and light.

Walk through the Sagrada Família, and you enter this language. Some symbols speak immediately, others whisper over time. Together they create an unbroken tapestry, drawing the eye, the mind, and the spirit into a story too vast for words alone.

CHAPTER 10

Gaudí's Vision Realized

The Sagrada Família rises over Barcelona much as Gaudí imagined it, a crown of towers, mosaic pinnacles shimmering in the Mediterranean sun, their shadows stretching long across the Eixample's ordered streets. More than a century after its foundation stone was laid, the basilica feels both ancient and new, a bridge between eras and a testament to patience.

Gaudí knew he would never see its completion. His vision was too ambitious for a single lifetime, and he accepted this with serenity. "My client," he said, "is not in a hurry." His work was to set the design so firmly in motion that it could outlast him, carried forward by others who understood its soul.

Today, cranes still move among the towers, their steel frames a reminder that this is a living work. Precision stonecutting machines shape the blocks, while skilled hands carve the final surfaces, a meeting of technology and craft that continues Gaudí's blend of innovation and tradition. The basilica remains self-funded, sustained by the millions who come each year to see, to pray, or simply to stand in wonder.

The nearing completion of the Jesus Christ Tower marks a turning point. When its cross is set in place, aligned to the four points of the compass and clad in ceramic and glass, it will become the tallest element of the basilica, yet still lower than Montjuïc hill, honoring Gaudí's conviction that no human work should surpass the height of God's creation.

For Barcelona, the Sagrada Família has long been more than architecture. It is a compass point, visible from the hills, the sea, and the city's heart. It has weathered wars, political shifts, and technological revolutions, growing steadily without losing the essence of its original vision.

When the last scaffolding is gone, the basilica will not simply be finished, it will continue to live. Light will keep changing across its façades, seasons will alter the quality of air in its nave, and visitors will keep discovering symbols they had not noticed before. Completion will be a milestone, not an ending.

Standing before it now, you see a work that began as sketches and plaster models and has become a cathedral of stone and light. It is Gaudí's vision realized: rooted in faith, shaped by human hands, and open to the sky, a gift to the city, the world, and the generations yet to come.

CHAPTER 11

Photographer's Map

The Sagrada Família changes with the light, and so do the photographs it yields. To capture it is not simply to point a camera; it is to follow the sun across stone and glass, to wait for the moment when shadow and color fall into harmony. Gaudí designed this building to move with the day, and the best images are those that move with it.

At dawn, the Nativity Façade glows in a warm gold. From the park across Carrer de la Marina, its reflection lies still in the pond, the carvings softened by the low light. The figures and foliage seem to emerge from the stone itself, alive in the gentle shadows.

By late afternoon, the Passion Façade comes into its own. Facing west, it gathers the amber light of sunset, its angular sculptures cut in deep relief. From the open square in Plaça de la Sagrada Família, you can frame its severity against the sinking sun, while the side streets offer sharper silhouettes.

The Glory Façade, facing south, is best seen at midday. Here the contrast between finished stone and scaffolding tells a truth no completed work can: that this is still a living building, caught between vision and completion.

Inside, light is the subject. Morning brings blues and greens through the eastern stained glass, spilling across the columns and pooling on the floor. Afternoon ignites the west in reds and golds, wrapping the nave in warmth. From the transept crossing, you can catch both spectrums meeting in the stone forest.

For interiors, a wide-angle lens reveals the full sweep of the nave and vaults, while a telephoto isolates the intimacy of detail, a capital carved like a plant, a pattern of color on stone, and the play of shadow in a branching column. Look directly upward from beneath the central skylight to see Gaudí's geometry distilled to its purest form.

The towers hold their own treasures. From within, narrow openings frame Barcelona like vertical postcards. At the pinnacles, mosaics blaze under the sun, and on clear days the sea stretches in a pale line at the horizon.

At night, the basilica shifts again. The façades are lit from below, their forms rising out of the darkness, and the star atop the Virgin Mary Tower glows against the sky. Long exposures from surrounding streets capture the stillness of stone in the flow of city lights.

The Sagrada Família is never the same twice. Each vantage, each hour, each change in weather rewrites its surfaces. The finest photographs do more than record what it looks like, they carry the memory of what it felt like to stand in its light.

EPILOGUE

The Eternal Work in Progress

The Sagrada Família stands as both a building and a parable, a reminder that some visions are too vast to be contained within the span of a single lifetime. Gaudí knew this. He accepted, even embraced, that his cathedral would be shaped by the hands, minds, and hearts of generations yet unborn. In this acceptance lies the quiet brilliance of his legacy: the idea that creation is a continuum, a living conversation between the past and the future, conducted in the medium of stone, glass, and light.

Walking away from the basilica, the sound of distant chisels still in your ears, you feel the paradox settle in. Here is a place at once unfinished and complete, a work forever in progress yet already capable of moving the soul. Its unfinished towers do not diminish it, they elevate it. They remind us that beauty is not only in what is done, but in what is still becoming.

The Sagrada Família is more than an icon of Barcelona or a testament to Gaudí's genius. It is a living organism. The sun's light through its stained glass shifts each hour, each season; the stone absorbs and reflects the moods of the day. And as construction cranes stand sentinel against the sky, the building teaches us an unspoken truth: that our lives, too, are cathedrals we build slowly, imperfectly, with each decision and act.

When the final stone is set, the Sagrada Família will no longer belong solely to the builders or the city. It will belong to the world, a completed dream rising from Catalan soil to touch the heavens. But until that day, it breathes in the present tense, a place where pilgrims, artists, and wanderers witness the marriage of faith and imagination in a perpetual dawn.

And so, as you leave its embrace, you carry a fragment of that dawn within you. For every step you take beneath the open sky is another stone laid in the cathedral of your own becoming.

ANTONI GAUDÍ

The Architect of God's Geometry

Antoni Gaudí i Cornet was born on 25 June 1852 in Reus, a sunlit Catalonian town where the Mediterranean's warmth met the rhythms of rural life. The son of a coppersmith, Gaudí grew up watching his father hammer, bend, and coax metal into forms that combined strength with beauty. From this artisan's workshop, he inherited not only a respect for craft but also an early fascination with the hidden geometry of creation.

A sickly child, Gaudí spent long periods in quiet observation. While other boys played, he traced the spirals of snail shells, studied the branching of trees, and marveled at the symmetry of leaves. These hours would shape his conviction that the truest architecture comes not from rigid blueprints, but from the living patterns of nature itself.

The Education of a Visionary

In 1868, Gaudí arrived in Barcelona to study architecture at the Provincial School of Architecture. His academic record was uneven, brilliance in design tempered by indifference to convention. Upon granting him his degree in 1878, the school's director remarked: *"We have given this academic title to either a fool or a genius. Time will tell."*

Time answered clearly. By his mid-twenties, Gaudí was designing works that blended Catalan craftsmanship with bold experimentation. Casa Vicens, Palau Güell, and other early commissions revealed his gift for merging local tradition with structural daring.

Nature as Blueprint

Gaudí did not simply decorate with natural motifs; he studied and applied the underlying laws that governed them. He created catenary arches that mirrored the curve of a hanging chain, parabolic vaults inspired by the path of falling water, and branching columns that distributed weight like the limbs of a tree. His models were made of strings, sandbags, and mirrors, humble tools for revealing nature's eternal equations.

The Sagrada Família – Faith in Stone

In 1883, Gaudí took over the design of the Basílica i Temple Expiatori de la Sagrada Família. Over the next four decades, he transformed it from a neo-Gothic concept into a living testament to divine order, a forest of stone, rising toward light. In his final 15 years, he devoted himself entirely to it, living in near monastic simplicity and working as if time itself were his collaborator. He believed its completion need not be hurried: *"My client,"* he said, *"is not in a hurry."*

Final Years and Passing

By the 1920s, Gaudí had become a solitary figure, wholly consumed by his work. On 7 June 1926, while walking to evening prayers, he was struck by a tram. Mistaken for a beggar due to his humble clothing, he received delayed care and died three days later. Barcelona buried him with the honor of a national treasure, placing him in the crypt of the Sagrada Família.

An Enduring Legacy

Gaudí's legacy is more than a collection of buildings; it is a philosophy that architecture should breathe, grow, and speak in the same language as the world that birthed it. His works remain UNESCO World Heritage Sites and sources of global wonder, continuing to inspire architects, artists, and pilgrims alike. The still-unfinished Sagrada Família rises as both his monument and his message: that true beauty serves not just the eye, but the soul.

THE ARCHITECTURAL LANGUAGE OF ANTONI GAUDÍ

Antoni Gaudí's architecture resists easy classification. Rooted in Gothic revival yet infused with the restless spirit of Catalan Modernisme, his work transforms stone, iron, and glass into forms that feel alive. It is neither anchored wholly in the past nor propelled entirely into the future; rather, it is an organic synthesis of nature's geometry, sacred symbolism, and engineering genius.

Nature as the Master Plan

For Gaudí, nature was not merely a source of inspiration, it was the ultimate designer. He studied the branching of trees, the spiral of seashells, the crystalline logic of snowflakes, and the fluidity of waves. These patterns shaped not only his ornamentation but his structures themselves. The branching columns of the Sagrada Família echo the load-bearing logic of tree trunks and boughs, marrying stability with grace. As he declared, *"Nothing is art if it does not come from nature."* In his buildings, natural form and structural function are one and the same.

Geometry in Motion

Gaudí's visual vocabulary was grounded in advanced geometry, ruled surfaces, helicoids, hyperboloids, paraboloids, and catenary arches. He often built chain-and-weight models to find the most stable curve under gravity, then inverted them to design arches of breathtaking strength and elegance. This scientific precision allowed his work to stand with resilience while appearing almost dreamlike.

Where Craft Meets Innovation

Gaudí honored the artisanal traditions of Catalonia, ceramics, wrought iron, carpentry, while boldly experimenting with materials and techniques. His celebrated *trencadís* mosaics, made from shards of broken tile, turned discarded fragments into vibrant, light-catching surfaces. He blurred the line between architect and craftsman, ensuring every balcony, handrail, and hinge carried his personal signature.

Light as a Living Element

In Gaudí's world, light was as vital as stone. He designed spaces to choreograph the sun's movement, using stained glass, skylights, and calculated angles to create patterns that shift with the hours and seasons. The result is architecture in constant dialogue with the sky, interiors that feel alive because they are never lit the same way twice.

Sacred Symbolism in Every Detail

Gaudí's architecture is steeped in Christian symbolism, but it is symbolism made tangible through nature's forms. His façades read like vast stone scriptures, biblical scenes intertwined with organic motifs, each figure and frieze part of a larger theological narrative. Yet his symbolism avoids heaviness; it invites contemplation, leading the observer from the visible to the transcendent.

A Unified Vision

Above all, Gaudí's genius lay in his ability to unify. He conceived his projects as total works of art, controlling every detail from the structural frame to the smallest ornamental element. In the Sagrada Família, this unity reaches its fullest expression, an immersive synthesis of architecture, sculpture, light, and sound, designed not merely to shelter the faithful but to lift the soul.

In the end, Gaudí's style is not a formula to be imitated but a philosophy to be absorbed: that architecture can grow like a living organism, speak in the language of nature, and point, quietly yet powerfully, toward the divine.

BARCELONA

City of Light, Sea, and Stone

Barcelona is a city that refuses to be seen all at once. It is a shifting mosaic, sunlit mornings spilling over grand avenues, amber evenings softening the edges of Gothic spires, and bursts of color curling across facades in the playful curves of Modernisme. Here, history and invention share the same streets, speaking in the same breath.

The Mediterranean is always close, its salt-laced breeze drifting through the Ramblas, mingling with the scent of strong coffee and fresh bread. In the Barri Gòtic and El Born, stones laid by Romans and shaped by medieval masons still hold the echo of centuries. Yet just beyond, there is the boldness of a culture unafraid of risk: buildings that ripple like waves, ironwork that curls like vines, mosaics that seem plucked from dreams.

And in the heart of it all, the Sagrada Família rises, a living paradox of audacity and humility. It belongs wholly to Barcelona, yet stands apart from it, as if some fragment of heaven chose this city as its anchor. Gaudí's unfinished basilica is no mere landmark; it is Barcelona's heartbeat and its question mark, forever asking what beauty might emerge when nature, faith, and human imagination are set free.

From afar, its towers appear like a skyline of their own, delicate as lace and unyielding as mountains. Up close, the building reveals the soul of the city itself: rooted in tradition, yet endlessly inventive; shaped by history, yet always becoming. Even the cranes that pierce its silhouette seem less like interruptions and more like symbols, that here, creation is an ongoing act, never truly complete.

To know Barcelona is to walk this balance between the old and the daring, the still and the in-progress. And to stand before the Sagrada Família is to understand the city's truest secret: that it is not only a place to be visited, but a living work of art, always in motion, always in light.

CATALONIA

Land Between Mountains and Sea

Barcelona is more than a city, it is the beating heart of Catalonia, a region in Spain's northeast where the Pyrenees rise like ancient sentinels and the Mediterranean glitters in endless blue. This is a land of striking contrasts: wind-bent pines on rugged coastal cliffs, sunlit vineyards spilling down golden hillsides, and deep mountain valleys where rivers carve their way toward the sea.

Catalonia speaks in its own language, Catalan, and carries a cultural identity as layered and enduring as the stone of its medieval villages. Roman aqueducts still stride across the countryside, Gothic spires pierce the skyline, and cutting-edge design studios hum with modern creativity. In the kitchens, the region's geography becomes a feast: earthy stews from the mountains, seafood caught with the morning tide, vegetables kissed by Mediterranean sun.

Barcelona gathers all these influences into one vibrant mosaic. The wild energy of the Pyrenees finds its echo in the city's art, the colors of the Costa Brava reappear in its architecture, and the generosity of its fertile plains spills into its bustling markets. This is a city that has always looked outward, to traders, travelers, and dreamers, yet holds fast to the proud traditions of its land.

Within this rich tapestry, one creation rises above all others: the Sagrada Família. It is at once a child of Catalonia, born from its stone, its light, its spirit, and a vision that belongs to the world. Standing in the heart of Barcelona, it gathers the essence of the region into a single, soaring form: rooted in the earth, reaching for the sky.

SPAIN

A Land of Many Worlds

Spain is a country of dazzling variety, a living mosaic of landscapes, languages, and legacies. From the snow-dusted peaks of the Sierra Nevada to the sun-baked plains of Castile, from Galicia's wild Atlantic cliffs to Andalusia's languid olive groves, each region beats with its own pulse and poetry.

It is a nation of many tongues, Spanish (Castilian), Catalan, Basque, and Galician, each carrying centuries of verse, politics, and pride. Its cities gleam with architectural wonders: the Moorish lacework of Granada's Alhambra, the Renaissance grace of Salamanca, and the modernist curves of Barcelona. In the villages, time still follows the rhythm of the sun: afternoon's slow, festivals spill into cobbled streets, and tradition dances easily alongside modern life.

Spain's history is a long conversation between cultures. Romans left their aqueducts, Visigoths their churches, Moors their gardens and palaces. Catholic monarchs bound kingdoms together, explorers carried its flag across oceans, and the modern age brought artists, writers, and architects whose work would shape the world's imagination.

Life here is not merely lived, it is savored. Food is a shared celebration: saffron paella, fresh seafood by the coast, small plates of tapas passed among friends. Music and dance are languages of the soul, whether in the aching cry of flamenco or the playful rhythm of a street percussionist.

And in Barcelona, in the proud and distinct region of Catalonia, rises a creation that gathers all these threads, history, art, nature, and faith, into stone: the Sagrada Família. This basilica belongs not only to the city but to the very story of Spain, embodying the nation's centuries-old conversation between tradition and innovation, and standing as a living testament to one man's dream, still unfolding beneath the Mediterranean light.

APPENDIX A

Visual Glossary

The Sagrada Família is rich in architectural language and symbolic detail. Understanding its terms is like learning the grammar of Gaudí's vision , it allows you to read the basilica more deeply, whether you are studying its structure or simply standing in awe beneath its towers.

Apse — The semicircular or polygonal recess at the eastern end of a church, usually behind the altar. In the Sagrada Família, the apse is crowned by towers dedicated to the apostles and decorated with intricate sculptural work.

Ambulatory — The curved walkway around the back of the altar and apse, allowing movement without disturbing the central liturgical space. Gaudí lined it with chapels and symbolic ornament.

Baldachin — A canopy-like structure above the altar. In the basilica, it hangs like a crown suspended in light, echoing natural forms.

Capital — The decorative top of a column. In Gaudí's nave, capitals transition from geometric shapes into branching forms, supporting the vaults above like the tops of trees.

Catenary Arch — An arch shaped like the curve of a hanging chain. Gaudí used this naturally efficient form for strength and elegance throughout the basilica.

Clerestory — The high section of wall containing windows above eye level, flooding the nave with light that shifts in mood and tone throughout the day.

Façade — The main exterior face of a building. The basilica's three façades, Nativity, Passion, and Glory, each convey a chapter of the Christian story through sculpture and form.

Hyperboloid — A curved surface made from straight lines. Gaudí used this form in skylights and vaults to direct light and distribute weight.

Liturgical East/West — In church tradition, "east" refers to the altar end and "west" to the main entrance. The Nativity Façade faces east, the Passion Façade west.

Mosaic Pinnacle — The decorative top of a tower, covered in colorful ceramic pieces. These crown the evangelist and apostle towers, catching sunlight by day and glowing when lit at night.

Nave — The central aisle of a church where the congregation gathers. In the basilica, the nave is a stone forest, with tall branching columns.

Rose Window — A large circular stained glass window. The basilica's rose windows pour color into the interior, adding to its shifting light.

Spires — Tapered towers rising above the façades. Each of Gaudí's spires bears symbolic ornament and mosaic work, representing saints or theological themes.

Stained Glass — Colored glass set into windows, arranged in patterns or images. In the Sagrada Família, stained glass shapes the light from cool morning blues to warm evening reds.

Transept — The arms of a cross-shaped church that intersect the nave. The basilica's transepts are crowned by towers and open to expansive interior views.

Vault — An arched ceiling or roof. Gaudí's vaults are supported by branching columns, creating the impression of a canopy.

Viticulture Symbolism — Use of grapevine motifs, symbolizing both natural abundance and the Eucharist.

Zoömorphic Ornament — Decorative sculpture based on animals. Lizards, birds, and other creatures appear throughout the basilica, blending nature and faith.

These terms are keys to reading the basilica's form and meaning. With them, the details in the chapters, and in the plates that follow, will speak more clearly, revealing the layers of thought and artistry in Gaudí's unfinished masterpiece.

APPENDIX B

Timeline & Milestones

The story of the Sagrada Família is a saga of vision, persistence, and devotion, stretching over more than a century. These are the moments that shaped it.

1882 - The Foundation Stone
Construction begins under Francisco de Paula del Villar in a traditional Gothic Revival style. The foundation stone is laid on March 19, the Feast of St. Joseph.

1883 - Gaudí Takes the Helm
At just 31, Antoni Gaudí assumes leadership, radically reimagining the design into a blend of nature-inspired forms, structural daring, and profound Christian symbolism.

1892–1893 - The Nativity Façade Rises
Work begins on the Nativity Façade, its sculptural program bursting with botanical, animal, and biblical detail.

1925 - First Tower Completed

The bell tower dedicated to St. Barnabas crowns the Nativity Façade, the basilica's first true landmark in Barcelona's skyline.

1926 - Gaudí's Death

On June 10, Gaudí dies after being struck by a tram. He is buried in the crypt, leaving only a fraction of his vision complete.

1936 - Civil War Destruction

During the Spanish Civil War, fire damages the crypt and destroys much of Gaudí's workshop, including original models.

1954–1976 - Passion Façade Emerges

Work resumes after decades of slow progress. The stark, angular Passion Façade is constructed, in deliberate contrast to the ornate Nativity side.

1976 - Four Passion Towers Completed

The quartet of towers on the Passion Façade reshapes Barcelona's horizon.

1980s–1990s - Interior Transformation

Focus shifts inside. The forest-like columns rise, vaults take shape, and stained glass floods the space with color.

2010 - Consecration as Basilica

On November 7, Pope Benedict XVI consecrates the Sagrada Família. Worship fills the nave for the first time.

2016 - Glory Façade Begins

Work starts on the grand western façade, the most ambitious and symbolically dense of all.

2020 - Global Pause

The COVID-19 pandemic halts construction, the first such pause since the Civil War.

Projected 2030s - Completion

When the final towers and the Glory Façade are complete, the basilica will be the tallest church in the world, fulfilling Gaudí's dream in stone, glass, and light.

Closing Note

Each milestone is not just an architectural event but a step in a long act of devotion, a reminder that the Sagrada Família is as much about the patience of creation as the structure itself.

SOURCES & CITATIONS

Books & Monographs

- Bassegoda Nonell, Joan. *El Gran Gaudí*. Ediciones Ceac, 2002.
- Cirici, Alexandre. *Gaudí: La Biografía de un Genio*. Ediciones Polígrafa, 1996.
- Descharnes, Robert, and Clovis Prevost. *Gaudí: The Visionary*. Taschen, 2003.
- Martinell, César. *Gaudí: Su Vida, Su Teoría, Su Obra*. Editorial Blume, 1967.
- Zerbst, Rainer. *Antoni Gaudí: The Complete Buildings*. Taschen, 2014.

Academic & Historical References

- Collins, George R. "The Design and Construction of the Sagrada Família." *Journal of the Society of Architectural Historians*, vol. 24, no. 1, 1965, pp. 15–33.
- Flores, Carlos. *Arquitectura Española Contemporánea*. Editorial Blume, 1989.
- Puig Boada, Isidre. *El Pensamiento de Gaudí*. Asociación de Amigos de Gaudí, 2000.

Official & Institutional Sources

- *Sagrada Família Official Website.* https://sagradafamilia.org , Official history, architectural plans, and current construction updates.
- UNESCO World Heritage Centre. *Works of Antoni Gaudí* (Inscription No. 320bis). https://whc.unesco.org
- Ajuntament de Barcelona (Barcelona City Council). *Patrimoni Arquitectònic de Barcelona.*

Newspapers & Magazines

- "Gaudí's Sagrada Família: The Final Stages of an Endless Masterpiece." *The Guardian*, 19 Oct. 2021.
- "Barcelona's Beloved Basilica Nears Completion." *National Geographic*, May 2022.
- "The Mathematics Behind Gaudí's Curves." *Scientific American*, June 2011.

Photography & Visual References

- Arxiu Mas (Institut Amatller d'Art Hispànic), Barcelona, Historic photographs of Gaudí's works.
- Brangulí Archives, Barcelona.
- Image plates commissioned exclusively for this edition, created by professional architectural photographers with full reproduction rights secured.

FURTHER READING & EXPLORATION

For those inspired to journey deeper into the mind of Antoni Gaudí, the Sagrada Família, and the cultural spirit of Barcelona, these books, resources, and experiences have been chosen for their accuracy, depth, and ability to enrich your understanding.

Books & In-Depth Studies

- Rainer Zerbst – *Antoni Gaudí: The Complete Buildings* (Taschen, 2014) , A lavishly illustrated survey covering every work, with detailed explanations and stunning photography.
- Joan Bassegoda Nonell – *El Gran Gaudí* (Ediciones Ceac, 2002) , A scholarly Spanish-language biography offering rare insights into Gaudí's philosophy and methods.
- Gijs van Hensbergen – *Gaudí* (HarperCollins, 2001) , An accessible and engaging narrative blending biography with the story of modern Barcelona.
- George R. Collins – *Antonio Gaudí* (George Braziller, 1960) , A classic text examining Gaudí's architectural language and innovative forms.

Academic Papers & Scholarly Perspectives

- *The Design and Construction of the Sagrada Família*, George R. Collins, *Journal of the Society of Architectural Historians*, Vol. 24, No. 1 (1965).
- *Mathematics in Nature: Gaudí's Geometric Forms*, Various authors, *Mathematics and Architecture Journal*.

Museums & Key Institutions

- Gaudí House Museum, Once Gaudí's residence in Park Güell, now a curated space with original furniture and models.
- Museu Nacional d'Art de Catalunya (MNAC), Contextualizes Gaudí's era within Catalonia's artistic heritage.
- Col·legi d'Arquitectes de Catalunya, Regular exhibitions and archives dedicated to Gaudí's work and influence.

Digital & Interactive Resources

- Official Sagrada Família Website, sagradafamilia.org: Construction updates, virtual tours, and detailed explanations of each element.
- UNESCO World Heritage Listing, whc.unesco.org: Official recognition and heritage documentation for Gaudí's works.
- Google Arts & Culture – Antoni Gaudí Collection, High-resolution images, 3D models, and interactive essays.

On-Site Exploration & Walking Routes

- *Ruta del Modernisme*, A mapped walking route through Barcelona's Modernist gems, including multiple Gaudí masterpieces.
- Sagrada Família Tower Visit, For unmatched views of the basilica's details and the Barcelona skyline.

ABOUT THE AUTHOR

Pranav Pandya is an entrepreneur and writer with a deep reverence for the sacred masterpieces that have shaped human history. His work explores the meeting place between legend, devotion, and the enduring presence of places where faith and artistry meet.

In *SAGRADA FAMÍLIA: Stone, Light, and Gaudí's Unfinished Masterpiece – Inside Barcelona's Most Extraordinary Basilica*, Pranav offers an immersive journey into one of the world's most awe-inspiring creations, tracing how Antoni Gaudí's vision fused engineering, symbolism, and divine aspiration into a living cathedral. With luminous storytelling and a photographer's eye for detail, he brings to life not only the basilica's soaring towers and radiant stained glass, but also the centuries of craft, dedication, and spiritual yearning embedded in every stone.

When not writing, Pranav can often be found visiting sacred edifices, delving into history, or exploring nature parks with his trusty camera, capturing wildlife, birds, and landscapes that mirror the enduring wonder of the natural world.

VISUAL PLATES

Plate 1 – The Nativity Façade at Dawn

As the first light of morning spills over Barcelona, the Nativity Façade awakens in a wash of soft gold. The rising sun ignites every fold of stone, catching on leaves, petals, feathers, and faces, until the façade seems to breathe. This eastern front, Gaudí's joyous tribute to Christ's birth, overflows with nature's abundance. Every plant and animal carved here is a species native to Catalonia, carefully chosen to affirm Gaudí's belief in the unity of all creation. The result is both a theological statement and a living stone garden, where faith and the natural world intertwine in radiant harmony.

Plate 2 – Gaudí's Original Model Fragments

Rescued from the rubble after the Spanish Civil War, these plaster fragments reveal the geometric genius behind the basilica's soaring forms. Gaudí used ruled surfaces and catenary arches to marry beauty with structural efficiency.

Plate 3 – Forest of Columns

Inside the nave, columns branch like trees, lifting the ceiling as a forest canopy. The change in stone color marks different load paths, a fusion of engineering and metaphor, grounding the worshipper while lifting the gaze heavenward.

Plate 4 – Passion Façade Shadows

Angular and stripped of ornament, this façade's stark lines and deep shadows reflect the suffering of Christ. Sculptor Josep Maria Subirachs embraced an almost cubist style to evoke anguish and sacrifice.

Plate 5 – Stained Glass, West Transept

Blues and greens dominate this side, capturing the cool light of evening. Gaudí designed the windows to be read like a chromatic clock, warm tones for sunrise and cool tones for sunset.

Plate 6 – The Crypt

The humble heart of the basilica, where Gaudí is buried. Romanesque curves and low light create a contemplative space, in stark contrast to the vertical drama above.

Plate 7 – The Glory Façade Model

Still under construction, this façade will be the most elaborate, representing the road to God through the Last Judgment and the beatific vision. The scale model shows its immense vertical thrust and complex symbolic layering.

Plate 8 – Bell Towers from Above

From a bird's-eye view, the towers spiral upward like stone organ pipes. Each tower is dedicated to an apostle and topped with colorful ceramic mosaics inspired by Mediterranean fruit.

Plate 9 – Light Well and Vaulting

The interplay between ribbed vaults and skylights creates an ever-changing lightscape, intended to mimic the dappled sunlight of a woodland path.

Plate 10 – Gaudí's Workshop Recreation

Reconstructed from surviving photographs, the workshop shows how Gaudí worked, hanging string models upside down to visualize gravity's pull, then inverting them to design arches.

Plate 11 – Night Illumination

Artificial lighting transforms the Sagrada Família into a beacon, its towers glowing like candles in the dark. This was never part of Gaudí's original plan, but it has become a signature of modern Barcelona.

Plate 12 – Completion Rendering

The digitally rendered vision of the completed basilica, all eighteen towers, façades, and decorative details in place. This image bridges the gap between dream and reality, offering a glimpse of the work's destined grandeur.

Printed in Dunstable, United Kingdom